A-Z INVENTORS WHO LOOK LIKE ME

Copyright @ 2018 iGLOW Consulting, Firm LLC and in partnership with iEsteemMe Academics. ™
Cover Design @2018 by Cameron Wilson

All rights reserved. No part of this book may be reproduced in any form or by electronic or mechanical mean, without written permission from its publisher.

@iglowconsulting
http://iesteemme.com
http://iglowconsulting.org
http://lifestyleintentionaltees.com

"I Am Because You Are, You Are Because I Am."   ISBN 978-1-795-79352-0

A-Z INVENTORS WHO LOOK LIKE ME
"I am because they are."

ABOUT THE BOOK

Children are shaped, influenced, and cultivated to believe things that are often times in misalignment with their genius. Meet 22 trailblazing women and men who broke barriers of racism, oppression, and repression to improve the lives of future generations, despite their living and working conditions. Through rhyme and colorful illustrations this book will inspire young readers to learn about their African American History, increase vocabulary, fluency, and unleash their tailor made purpose. They will grow, explore, and begin to create this for themselves. A-Z Inventors Who Look Like Me is important, timely, and written in a style that kids will enjoy. The assurance that they are the extension of African American inventors and are filled with talent, creativity, and passion is certain to help them build the confidence needed to discover, develop, and cultivate their strengths. We are all here for a purpose. We are contributors. We just need to see it, hear it, read it and believe it.

ABOUT THE AUTHOR
SPEAKER | EDUCATOR | TRANSFORMATION LIFESTYLE COACH Hazel Jay is a K-12 educator with over 20 years invested in building the esteem and confidence of children. Hazel teaches how children are shaped, influenced, and cultivated to believe things that are often times in misalignment with their genius. Hazel Jay is the CEO of iGLOW Consulting Firm, LLC and Founder of iGLOW Consulting and iEsteemMe Academics.

To all the children who need a reminder that their essence, soul and spirit are fearfully and wonderfully created.

A I am **ambitious** and **accomplished** because Augustus Jackson looks just like me. In 1879, he invented ice cream. Wow! He is great and I am too!

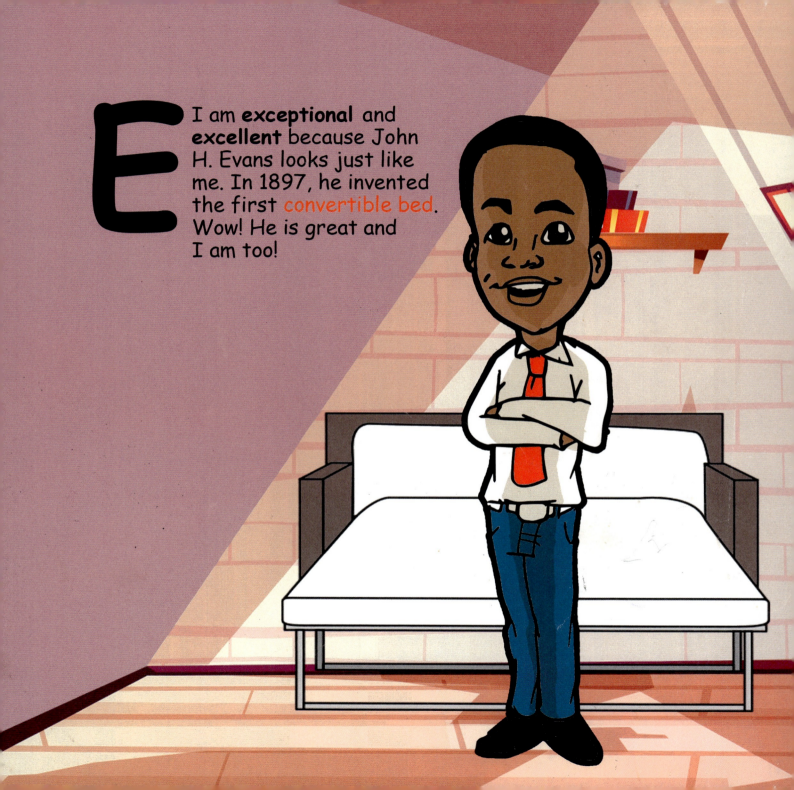

E I am **exceptional** and **excellent** because John H. Evans looks just like me. In 1897, he invented the first convertible bed. Wow! He is great and I am too!

F I am **fearless** and **fierce** because Robert F. Flemmings Jr. looks just like me. In 1886, he invented the first **guitar**. Wow! He is great and I am too!

L

I am **luxuriant** and **legendary** because John L. Love looks just like me. In 1897, he invented the first pencil sharpener. Wow! He is great and I am too!

P I am **powerful** and **persistent** because Anthony Phillis looks just like me. In 1991, he invented the first computer keyboard. Wow! He is great and I am too!

V I am a **valuable** and **vibrant** member of society because Simon Vincent looks just like me. In 1920, he invented the first woodworking machine. Wow! He is great and I am too!

W

I have potential. I am **wondrous** and **worthy** because Richardson, Williams looks just like me. In 1886, he invented the first **child's carriage**. Wow! He is great and I am too

X
Y
Z

Wow! How **eXhilarating** to know I am born with a bright future too. I am not too **young** to make an impact on the world. I will leave a positive imprint for my community. I have the **zeal** to persevere.

MOTTO:

I am empowered. I am inspired. I am motivated. I will be disciplined. I will wake up and pay attention with my mind, eyes, and ears because I am a child of African greatness.
I am a future scholar. Just like the African-American inventors who look like me I will continue to contribute to humanity through my genius.

"I am because we are and therefore we are because I am."
- Ashanti Proverb

Special Thanks...

To my Kindergarten Teacher, Mrs. Thomas, Gainesville FL.; 7th grade History Teacher, Mrs. Hodge and 8th grade Teacher, Mr. Arceneaux, Elmhurst Middle School, Oakland, CA.; Castlemont High Teachers 1993-1996, Oakland, CA.; Black Studies Department and Dr. Jamal Cooks, San Francisco State University, San Francisco, CA.; Dr. Price, Dr. Mahone and Urban Leadership Department 2007-2008; Dr. Judy Wesinger, Dr. Darcell, Mr. Bush, Lorry I Lokey School of Business, Oakland, CA; and all my family and friends, BSU 2002-2005, ASCENT African American Graduate Association 2013-2015. A special shout out to my church family, Greater Refugee Whittington Temple, Oakland CA., Family Bible Fellowship, Newark, CA., and Pastor Harris, New Life Community Church, Decatur, GA.

@iglowconsulting
http://iesteemme.com
http://iglowconsulting.org
http://lifestyleintentionaltees.com

___

"I Am Because You Are, You Are Because I Am"　　　　ISBN 978-1-720-15215-6

Made in the USA
Coppell, TX
28 November 2020